What's in this book

This book belongs to

_____

我喜欢水果 I like fruit

学习内容 Contents

沟通 Communication

说说喜欢吃什么、喝什么
Talk about what someone likes to eat and drink

问他人喜欢吃什么、喝什么
Ask about what someone likes to eat and drink

背景介绍：
厨房里，浩浩抱着布朗尼看着一大篮水果，
他们都很想吃。

生词 New words

★	喜欢	to like
★	吃	to eat
★	水果	fruit
★	喝	to drink
★	果汁	fruit juice
★	水	water
★	不	not, no
	苹果	apple
	香蕉	banana
	葡萄	grape

句式 Sentence patterns

我喜欢（喝）果汁。
I like fruit juice.

我喜欢（吃）苹果。
I like apples.

你喜欢吃什么？
What do you like to eat?

你喜欢喝什么？
What do you like to drink?

文化 Cultures

中国特产水果——荔枝
Chinese speciality fruit — lychee

跨学科学习 Project

统计哪种水果受欢迎，
画出图表
Conduct a survey on fruit
and make a pictogram

参考答案：
1 Apples/bananas/grapes are my favourite fruit.
2 Yes, I do. Fruit is good for our health./No, I do not.
I do not regularly eat fruit.
3 I think Brownie likes apples/bananas/grapes.

Get ready

1 What is your favourite fruit?

2 Do you eat fruit every day?

3 What fruit do you think Brownie likes?

故事大意：

浩浩一家人一起在客厅吃水果、喝果汁。浩浩想给布朗尼吃葡萄，爸爸及时提醒小狗不能吃葡萄。浩浩则因为吃饱了，也不能再吃了。

一般对于固体的食物，我们用"吃"。

chī
吃

shuǐ guǒ
水果

我喜欢吃水果。

参考问题和答案：

1 What are Hao Hao, Dad and Mum doing? (They are eating fruit while watching TV in the living room.)

2 Do you think Hao Hao likes to eat fruit? (Yes, there are various kinds of fruit on his plate.)

4

妈妈喜欢苹果，爸爸喜欢香蕉。

参考问题和答案：

1　What fruit do you think Mum likes to eat? (She likes to eat apples.)

2　What fruit do you think Dad likes to eat? (He likes to eat bananas.)

hē
喝
一般对于液体或流质的食物，
我们用"喝"。

guǒ zhī
果汁

shuǐ
水

姐姐喜欢喝果汁。

参考问题和答案：

1 What do you think Ling Ling likes? (She likes to drink fruit juice.)
2 Do you like to drink water or juice more? (I like to drink both.)

布朗尼，你喜欢吃什么？

参考问题和答案：

1 What do you think Brownie wants to do? (Brownie also wants to eat fruit.)
2 What is Hao Hao doing? (Hao Hao shows his plate to Brownie and asks Brownie what does it want to eat.)

bù

不

我们可以说"不"来
表示否定。

小心！ 小狗不能吃葡萄。

参考问题和答案：

1 What is Hao Hao doing? (Hao Hao is feeding Brownie grapes.)

2 Do you know why Dad looks so alarmed? (He wants to stop Hao Hao feeding Brownie. Because Brownie cannot eat grapes.)

8   3 Why Hao Hao looks so surprised? (Because he did not know that Brownie cannot eat grapes.)

你不能吃葡萄，我也不
吃了。

参考问题和答案：

1 Can Hao Hao and Brownie eat grapes? (No, they cannot.)
2 Why Hao Hao cannot eat grapes any more? (Because Hao Hao has eaten too much fruit.)

Let's think

1 **What do they like? Match the pictures to the people.**

提醒学生回忆故事，观察第4–7页。

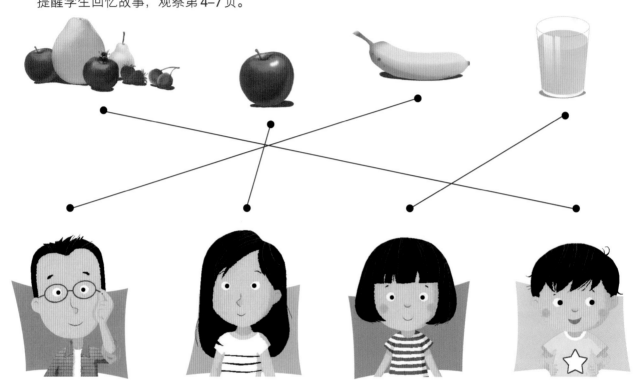

2 **Why can't Brownie eat grapes? Discuss with your friend.**

参考答案：
Brownie gets very ill if it eats grapes.

老师可以告诉学生，狗吃葡萄或葡萄干会引发中毒，此外，狗还不能吃巧克力、洋葱和酒等。养宠物时，我们应了解宠物的生活和饮食习惯，避免对它们造成伤害。此外，不管是宠物还是动物园里的动物，都不要随便喂食。

小心！小狗不能吃葡萄。

New words

1 Learn the new words.

延伸活动：
让学生运用所学词汇，用完整的一句话
来说说自己的情况："我喜欢（吃/喝）
……""我不喜欢（吃/喝）……"

喜欢　不　水　苹果　吃　水果　葡萄　喝　香蕉　果汁

2 Match the words to the pictures.
Write the letters.

a 吃　　b 喝　　c 水果
d 不喜欢　　e 喜欢

d

a

c

e

b

提醒学生注意区分液体食物用"喝"，固体食物用"吃"。

听听说说 Listen and say

1 Listen and decide. Put a tick or a cross.

2 Look at the pictures. Listen to the stor

第二题参考问题和答案：

1 How does Mum ask what would you like to eat/drink in Chinese? (你喜欢吃 / 喝什么？)

2 Do you know what fruit your friend/mum/dad likes best? (Grapes are my best friend's favourite fruit./My mum's favourite fruit is apples./My dad loves bananas best.)

第三题延伸活动：
基于本题的图片和句子，让学生以玲玲的身份来改写并说出句子。

...nd say.

你喝什么？

我喝果汁，谢谢。

你喜欢吃什么？

我不吃了。

3 Complete the sentences and say.

1

我们喜欢吃…… 水果

2

这是我的…… 葡萄

3

那是姐姐的…… 苹果

4

你……吃什么水果？ 喜欢

Task
告诉学生水果对我们的身体有益，我们应多吃些。同时，我们还可以加些创意，使水果变得更加有趣，如用苹果当做饮品杯、用苹果和葡萄做成蜘蛛、用香蕉做成鸟。

Count and write the number of fruit on each plate. Tell your friend.
提醒学生按某一特定顺序数，如从上到下，从左到右，会不容易数错。

苹果：____8____

苹果：____2____

葡萄：____30____

香蕉：____5____

Game
学生3-4人一组，一人说出问题，另一人回答并询问下一人。以此类推，循环问答。

Play a relay game.

这是什么水果？

这是香蕉。我喜欢吃香蕉。这是什么水果？

这是……我喜欢吃……这是什么水果？葡萄；葡萄

……

Song

🎧05 **Listen and sing.**

延伸活动：
老师让学生画出歌词中的水果，并将画纸贴在身上，分小组唱歌，唱到水果名称时，指出同学身上相应的水果。

喜欢吃水果吗？

苹果、香蕉和葡萄，

你喜欢吃什么？

喜欢喝果汁吗？

苹果汁、葡萄汁，

你喜欢喝什么？

课堂用语 Classroom language

拿出铅笔。
Take out a pencil.

拿出橡皮。
Take out a rubber.

学中文。
Learn Chinese.

写一写 Write

1 Learn and trace the stroke. 老师示范笔画动作，学生跟着做：用手在空中画出"提"。

提

2 Learn the component. Trace ⺡ in the characters.

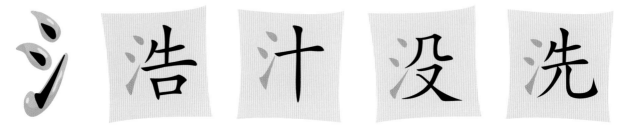

⺡ 浩 汁 没 洗

提醒学生"三点水"像是三滴落下的水滴。

3 Circle the characters with ⺡ .

提醒学生注意区分部件"三点水"和"两点水"。它们一般在字的左边，"三点水"像三滴水滴，多与"水"有关。"两点水"像冰的花纹，多与冰、寒冷有关。此外，"四点底"位于字的底部，是燃烧的火堆，多与"火"有关。

河　凉　点　燕　渠　浩　冰　海　热　照　汉　冷

4 Trace and write the character.

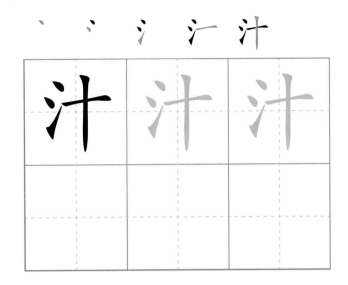

Over 3,000 years ago, Chinese characters were carved on bones. They looked like pictures.

Learn how the character for *water* has changed into the character we see today.

"水"原指岩壁上落下的水滴。后来"岩壁"简化成一竖，四周的笔画表示水滴。

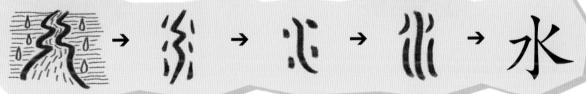

Can you guess the meaning of the character below?

It means the fruits on the tree.

"果"即树上长了果子。用"木"表示树，上方的表示果子。

Look	Draw	Write

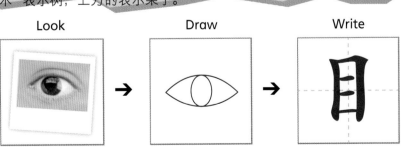

Follow the instructions.

先让学生简单地画出眼睛，再根据所画的图形想一想，和哪个已学的汉字最像。

"目"即人的单只眼睛，后随着字形发展竖写。

Cultures

1 Have you seen this fruit before?

This is a lychee, a summer fruit with a sweet flavour. It is grown in Southern China and has a history of over 2,000 years.

唐代唐明皇为博杨贵妃一笑，让人骑快马将荔枝从岭南送到长安。

2 Find your favourite fruit and tell your friend the harvest months.

建议问答句式："你喜欢吃什么水果？""我喜欢吃……月的……"。
较难的水果名称可以用英文说出。

一月	二月	三月	四月	五月	六月
石榴	柚子	木瓜	菠萝	草莓	荔枝

七月	八月	九月	十月	十一月	十二月
桃子	苹果	哈密瓜	梨	柿子	香蕉

1 **What fruit is popular in your class? Write the numbers and say.** 老师先和学生一起温习水果的名称，再由学生自主做调查。

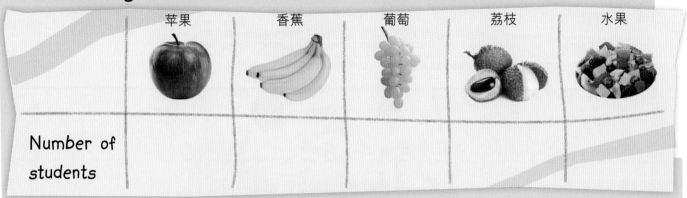

	苹果	香蕉	葡萄	荔枝	水果
Number of students					

2 **Colour the fruit survey pictogram. Discuss with your friend.**

告诉学生调查结果可以用图表来表达，图表可以更清晰、直观地表达信息，并方便做比较。提醒学生先根据调查结果给相应的水果数量涂色，再用自己的话来总结图表内容。

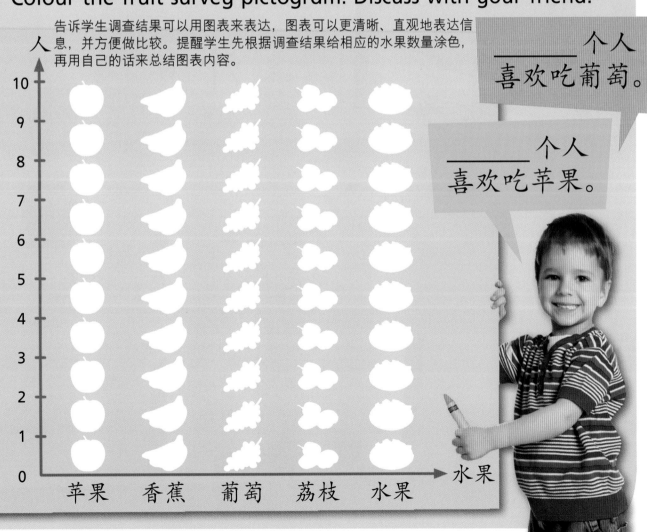

_____个人喜欢吃葡萄。

_____个人喜欢吃苹果。

温习 Checkpoint

1 Play the board game by starting from the bottom. Answer in Chinese.

Tell the Monkey King:

我……吃……

我喜欢吃水果。

Finish

Circle the component for 'water'.

浩浩

河

Write the character.

果 汁

你喜欢喝水吗？
我（不）喜欢喝水。

这是什么？
这是葡萄。

这是什么？
这是香蕉。

这是什么？
这是苹果。

这是什么？
这是水果。

Start

这是什么？
这是果汁。

评核方法：

学生两人一组，互相考察评价表内单词和句子的听说读写。交际沟通部分由老师朗读要求，学生再互相对话。如果达到了某项技能要求，则用色笔将星星或小辣椒涂色。

2 Work with your friend. Colour the stars and the chillies.

Words	说	读	写
喜欢	☆	☆	🌶
吃	☆	☆	🌶
水果	☆	☆	🌶
喝	☆	☆	🌶
果汁	☆	☆	🌶
水	☆	☆	🌶
不	☆	☆	🌶
苹果	☆	🌶	🌶
香蕉	☆	🌶	🌶
葡萄	☆	🌶	🌶

Sentences	说	读	写
我喜欢 (吃) 苹果。	☆	🌶	🌶
我喜欢 (喝) 果汁。	☆	☆	🌶
你喜欢吃什么？	☆	☆	🌶
你喜欢喝什么？	☆	☆	🌶

Talk about what someone likes eating and drinking	☆
Ask about what someone likes eating and drinking	☆

3 What does your teacher say?

评核建议：

根据学生课堂表现，分别给予"太棒了！(Excellent!)"、"不错！(Good!)"或"继续努力！(Work harder!)"的评价，再让学生圈出左侧对应的表情，以记录自己的学习情况。

My teacher says ...

分享 Sharing

延伸活动：
1 学生用手遮盖英文，读中文单词，并思考单词意思；
2 学生用手遮盖中文单词，看着英文说出对应的中文单词；
3 学生两人一组，尽量运用中文单词分角色复述故事。

Words I remember

喜欢	xǐ huan	to like
吃	chī	to eat
水果	shuǐ guǒ	fruit
喝	hē	to drink
果汁	guǒ zhī	fruit juice
水	shuǐ	water
不	bù	not, no
苹果	píng guǒ	apple
香蕉	xiāng jiāo	banana
葡萄	pú tao	grape

Other words

布朗尼	bù lǎng ní	Brownie, name of a dog
小心	xiǎo xīn	be careful
小狗	xiǎo gǒu	puppy
能	néng	can
也	yě	also, too
荔枝	lì zhī	lychee

OXFORD
UNIVERSITY PRESS

Oxford University Press is a department of the University of Oxford.
It furthers the University's objective of excellence in research, scholarship,
and education by publishing worldwide. Oxford is a registered trade mark of
Oxford University Press in the UK and in certain other countries

Published in Hong Kong by
Oxford University Press (China) Limited
39th Floor, One Kowloon, 1 Wang Yuen Street, Kowloon Bay,
Hong Kong

Illustrated by Anne Lee and Wildman

Photographs for reproduction permitted by Dreamstime.com

China National Publications Import & Export (Group) Corporation is an authorized distributor of
Oxford Elementary Chinese.

Please contact content@cnpiec.com.cn or 86-10-65856782

ISBN: 978-0-19-082142-5

10 9 8 7 6 5 4 3 2

Teacher's Edition
ISBN: 978-0-19-082154-8

10 9 8 7 6 5 4 3 2